Second Stride

present

hotel

In a room anything can happen

Words CARYL CHURCHILL   Music ORLANDO GOUGH

Direction/Choreography IAN SPINK   Design LUCY BEVAN

13 Singers, 2 dancers, 3 instrumentalists and eight rooms in a hotel

hotel

Text	Caryl Churchill
Music	Orlando Gough
Director/Choreographer	Ian Spink
Designer	Lucy Bevan

Production Manager	Paul O'Leary
Company Stage Manager	Lily Mollgaard
Technical Manager	Chris Clay
Deputy Stage Manager	David Marsland
Director's Assistant	Cass Fleming

Set built by	Creative Construction
Poster/leaflet design	MGA
Photographs	Richard Dean

There will be an interval between **Eight Rooms** and **Two Nights**

Hotel was premiered at the Schauspielhaus Hannover on 15th April 1997

Second Stride would like to thank the following for their help with this production: Philbeach Hotel, Earls Court.

Thank you for their work on the original work-in-progress: Rebecca Askew, Anton Browne, Daniela Clynes, Michael Dore, Angela Elliott, Louise Field, Carol Grimes, Eleanor Grynwasser, Mike Henry, Julien Jolly, Jenny Miller, Melanie Pappenheim, Christina Payne, Ian Shaw, Michele Smith.

For Second Stride
Toynbee Studios, 28 Commercial Street, London E1 6LS (0171 247 8917)

Artistic Director	Ian Spink
General Manager	Natalie Sinnadurai
Marketing/Press	Guy Chapman Associates (0171 242 1882)

Second Stride is supported by the Arts Council of England and for Hotel's visit to Germany by the British Council.

Second Stride is a registered charity number 328178

Hotel has been made possible with grants from The Britten-Pears Foundation and The Alan and Sheila Diamond Charitable Trust and donations from Mr Jack R Blair, Mr Nigel HM Chancellor, Sir Anthony Cleaver, Mrs Pauline Hyde and Prof. Graham Richards

Funded by THE ARTS COUNCIL OF ENGLAND

The British Council

eight rooms

TV ⎫	Angela Elliott
Ghost ⎭	
Silent woman	Gabrielle McNaughton
Silent man	Colin Poole
US woman	Daniela Clynes
US man	Mick O'Connor
Affair woman	Jenny Miller
Affair man	Richard Chew
Old French woman	Marjorie Keys
Old French man	Andrew Bolton
Gay woman (1)	G T Nash
Gay woman (2)	Rebecca Askew
Drunk woman	Carol Grimes
Drunk man	D W Matzdorf
Birdbook woman	Louise Field
Business man	Wayne Ellington

two nights

Man	Colin Poole
Woman	Gabrielle McNaughton
A diary found in a hotel room	Rebecca Askew, Andrew Bolton, Richard Chew, Daniela Clynes, Wayne Ellington, Angela Elliott, Louise Field, Carol Grimes, Marjorie Keys, D W Matzdorf, Jenny Miller, G T Nash, Mick O'Connor
Music Director/Piano	Walter Fabeck
Piano	Alex Maguire
Double bass	Sarah Homer

eight rooms

I kept thinking about a lot of different stories all happening on stage at once. How to cope with all those people talking at the same time? Easily of course if they're not talking but singing, and in any case I wanted to write an opera for Orlando. At some point I had the idea of a hotel where we'd see all the identical rooms superimposed as one room, all the people in the same space. And what sort of words should they sing? When I'm listening to sung words I like taking their meaning in without any effort, and I'm also happy to hear them just as sound. What I don't like is feeling I may be missing something important if I don't follow every word. What do I want from words in an opera? A situation, an emotion, an image. Some of the sections that had stayed with me most from **Lives of the Great Poisoners** (a 1991 piece with Orlando and Ian) had very simple words that could be taken in quickly and repeated. The little opera scene in **The Skriker** (1994, music Judith Weir) had words without the usual structure of sentences (welcome homesick drink drank drunk) but it was easy to understand what was happening. So in **Hotel,** how little need the characters say to let us know enough about them? I decided there would be no complete sentences, just little chunks of what was said or thought, that could be absorbed first time round or in a repeat or even never.

two nights

In Eight Rooms each of the thirteen singers is a different character; in Two Nights they all sing a diary that has been left in a hotel room. The silent performers in Eight Rooms now play two people who spend different nights in the same room. We want this piece to start from ideas about the choreography and Ian maps out the two stories, though the first thing to be set is the words, then the music, and the details of the choreography are to be worked out in rehearsal. Both the characters disappear in different ways, and the diary is written by someone who becomes invisible. What might be in a diary apart from how the body begins to vanish? Notes about other kinds of disappearance. On the internet I found worry about cities disappearing in smog, a magician making a building disappear, a Canadian legal judgment about objects that go missing, an anarchist using disappearance rather than confrontation as a "logical radical option", and a spell for becoming invisible translated from Greek magical documents. Again I used few words, glimpses as we flick through someone else's diary.

Caryl Churchill

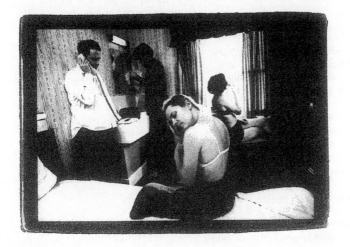

eight rooms

Caryl says What do you like
about opera?
I say The bits when everyone
sings at once.

So what about this? Caryl says:
one night in a hotel; eight rooms
are seen simultaneously. Excellent!
Off we go.

People sing duets, trios, quartets
with people they never meet. Their
lives intersect in the realm of
shared emotion, in the realm
of counterpoint and polyphony.

The action is everyday, consciously
undramatic.

Is it possible to write an opera
of everyday life? Isn't there an
inherent contradiction? Isn't the
function of opera to deal with
extremes of emotion? Should
not action resolve character?

A fragmentary libretto. Already a
move away from naturalism. Allows
me to compose the music, ie make
the text into music, rather than
being dragged along by the words.

A cyclic structure. The piece ends
almost as it began. A sense that
the next night would be similar.
We are interested in these people
only while they are in the hotel.
A crowd looked at from afar
(with occasional help of a pair
of binoculars).

Opera singers. NO!

Working with jazz singers. Should
I give opportunities to improvise?
Surely I am wasting their talent
if I don't ?... However, I am not
sure about this idea 'opportunities
to improvise'. If the music after
the improvised passage is not
affected by the improvisation,
then surely the improviser is just
filling in time?... I get very excited
by the idea of a completely
improvised opera, and then funk
it. Six months rehearsal would
be barely enough.

A lean, functional band: piano
duet and double bass. Almost like
a jazz rhythm section. A modest
but utterly crucial role. However,
the emotional energy must come
from the singers. Thirteen singers
and three players! – almost the
mirror image of many modern
chamber operas, where complex
texture is created with an
important role for the band and
the singers are treated almost
like instrumentalists.

two nights

A companion for Eight Rooms – not necessarily a friend. Same cast. What else happens in hotels? says Ian. A hotel is where you might go, for privacy, to do something lonely, radical, extreme, life changing, terminal.
Sid Vicious.

I want the music to be very different from Eight Rooms: the singers will be a choir.

A diary has been left in the room. The singers will sing the contents of the diary.

A kind of song cycle. Harmony rather than counterpoint. (Yikes, not my strong point.) Drama! Risk! A linear structure – a sense of not being able to retrace one's steps. Though one might want to. A much darker piece than Eight Rooms.

The dancers, who have had a peripheral role in Eight Rooms, are now centre stage. The singers... sing, and occasionally take part in the action.

The subject matter of Two Nights is definitely 'operatic'. But we haven't written an opera...

Should the dancing mimic the text? NO! Should it ignore the text? Not quite - it should connect, but on an emotional rather than literal level.

The old problem again: the text and the music are written in advance; the choreography can't exist until rehearsals start. How can the choreographer be expected to work with such an unbending structure? We consider scrapping the text and the music and making a devised piece (on the same theme) in rehearsal. An exhilarating and alarming idea. The singers' ability to improvise is a catalyst. We funk it. Cowards! Two months rehearsals needed, minimum.

You put so much emotion into singing your love songs, spend the evening pouring your heart out, but then go back to your hotel alone. k.d.lang [1]

To be inside that music, to be drawn into the circle of its repetitions: perhaps that is a place where one could finally disappear. Paul Auster – City of Glass [2]

1. Reproduced by kind permission of The Independent

2. reproduced by kind permission of Faber and Faber

Orlando Gough

eight rooms

two nights

began as a challenge. How do you fit fourteen hotel guests into one room? What happens when they all eventually go to bed? The potential for enormous traffic jams in such an intimate space seemed huge and fascinating. In rehearsal we were to discover that the simplest of acts, the cleaning of teeth, the hanging up of a dress, the reading of a magazine, demanded a relaxed yet rigorous precision when taking into account the thirteen other occupants of the space.

The hotel room channels many threads of action into a single stream of human experience covering a period of perhaps sixteen hours. Guests arrive, tiny incidents are briefly exposed; a drunken couple argue, a young woman dreams of a bird, an American plans a game of golf, a French couple drink tea, a business man rings home, two lovers whisper, a wife considers her marriage, a silent couple watch television. In one sense ordinary and unambiguous activities but collected together they produce a touching and mesmeric atmosphere. In the morning these people prepare to leave; a woman packs her case, a man comments on the weather, another orders breakfast, an insomniac finally succumbs to sleep. The sparse yet humane text combines with the music to produce a strangely uplifting piece of theatre.

Created some time later, **Two Nights** has become for me, an antidote to **Eight Rooms**. Here the challenge was, can you weave together three almost unrelated stories and play them out in the same location? The hotel room is now a more ambiguous, dangerous place, a catalyst for darker journeys, two of them danced, one of them sung to a sparkling counterpoint score. The singers have become a choral accompaniment and occasional extras to the choreographed action. A trapped woman struggles with her conscience and seeks salvation surrounded by strangers, a man haunted by his past is about to end his life. Their stories are danced out in extreme, dramatic bursts accompanied by entries from an abandoned diary, the diary of someone who has become invisible. The three self-contained threads playing simultaneously, are about magic, deception and transformation.

Ian Spink

EIGHT ROOMS

Characters

SILENT COUPLE
US COUPLE
AFFAIR COUPLE
OLD FRENCH COUPLE
GAY COUPLE
DRUNK COUPLE
BUSINESSMAN
BIRDBOOK WOMAN
TV
GHOST

Hotel bedroom. Large double bed, sink, wardrobe, TV.
It is eight identical hotel bedrooms superimposed.
Each couple behaves as if they were alone in the room.

1. Arrivals

SILENT COUPLE *arrive, start to settle in.*
BUSINESSMAN *arrives, puts on TV, flops on bed.*

TV
rain later . . heavier and more prolonged
on to tomorrow

US COUPLE *arrive.*

US MAN
which is terrific. The window you get a view of the

US WOMAN
uh huh uh huh

AFFAIR WOMAN *arrives alone.*
OLD FRENCH COUPLE *arrive.*

OLD COUPLE
demain . . le fleuve . . en bateau . . si tu veux

GAY COUPLE *arrive.*

GAY 1
I told him

GAY 2
you tell him

AFFAIR MAN *arrives.*

AFFAIR MAN
Miss me?

AFFAIR WOMAN
Missed you. Miss me?

AFFAIR MAN
Missed you.

BIRDBOOK WOMAN *arrives. Starts to read hotel brochure.*

BIRDBOOK WOMAN
The hotel is situated . .
in every room . .
continental or full English
in case of fire.

OTHERS *join in brochure.*

2. Settling In

BUSINESSMAN *phones home.*

BUSINESSMAN
Hi darling . . no really . . yeh . . yeh . . put him on.
Hi darling . . you did? . . big kiss, bye bye.
Hi darling . . you did? . . big kiss, bye bye.
Darling . . bye bye . . big kiss, bye bye.

GAY 1
we don't have to

GAY 2
of course we don't

GAY 1
we can simply

GAY 2
spend some time

GAY 1
get to know each other

GAY 2
get to know each other?

GAY 1
again.

US MAN
Golf in the neighbourhood . .

little guy in reception made me laugh when he said . .
if we get an early night we can make an early . .

US WOMAN
uh huh uh huh uh huh

OLD COUPLE
son chapeau

They laugh.

AFFAIR COUPLE
can't believe
just so
nothing like
wonder

BIRDBOOK WOMAN *is reading a bird book*

BIRDBOOK WOMAN
sparrowhawk . . tinted eggs . . sedges . . nightingale

DRUNK COUPLE *arrive cheerful and noisy.*

because I really sincerely do
you're completely right to
and he's such an arsehole
which nobody understands except you

3. TV

By now many people are lying on the bed watching TV,
often changing channels.

TV
your mother's very upset . . further consultation . . returns to
feed her young . . *in* London . .

VIEWERS
turn over turn over

BUSINESSMAN *reads a book.*

BUSINESSMAN
raced towards him . . headless . . blood on his

OLD WOMAN *reads a book.*

OLD WOMAN
longtemps soulagé. . son beau visage . .

4. Sleep

Most of them are in bed by now.

BIRDBOOK WOMAN *reads.*

BIRDBOOK WOMAN
Care charmer sleep son of the sable night . .
and let the day be time enough to mourn . .
and never wake to feel the day's disdain.

GAY COUPLE *and* AFFAIR COUPLE *quartet*

your eyes
do you like?
this is so
my angel
skin
so wet
further and further
always

5. Quarrel

DRUNK COUPLE *quarrel loudly.*

what the hell do you think
shut up shut up
just say that again just
out get out
don't you dare
always knew
kill you
never

OTHERS *are alarmed by the noise.*

shall we phone the desk?
shall we bang on their door?
are they hurting each other?
shut the fuck up

*The drunk couple are exhausted, the quarrel ends,
everyone settles down again.*

TV
not quite far enough down the table
35 . . 42 . . 43 . .

TV is turned off.

6. Insomnia

Care charmer sleep continues.

INSOMNIAC (GAY 2)

I'm I'm afraid I'm afraid I I'm afraid I can't
I'm afraid I can't sleep
I'm afraid I can't sleep afraid I can't sleep
I can't sleep can't sleep sleep

7. Obsessive

US MAN *gets up quietly. All is quiet except insomniac.*

He does ritual movements. He keeps stopping and going back to the beginning.

US WOMAN *wakes up.*

US WOMAN
What?

US MAN
Honey.

US WOMAN
What you doing?

US MAN
Honey.

US WOMAN
Come to bed.

US MAN
Honey.

He goes back to bed, seems to sleep.

8. Lonely

US WOMAN
hold you close because I'm lonely
are you there? because I'm lonely
when I hold you close it makes me lonely
never close   never there
lonely

GAY 2 *has been continuing insomniac song. Now sings*
with US WOMAN.

afraid and lonely
can't sleep and lonely
hold you close because I'm lonely
I wish I was with
afraid I can't sleep
lonely

9. Anguish

AFFAIR WOMAN *wakes up.*

AFFAIR WOMAN
afraid I can't sleep
how I miss
what if I lose
danger danger
children in danger
gone what if they're gone what if

AFFAIR MAN *wakes and soothes her.*

hush hush hush

10. Dreams

GAY 1 *is dreaming.*

walking down the road I saw a
car who is a man who is a
flying down the hill I saw a
bird who is a meeting of the
doctors of the house who is a
cupboard with a cat who is a
mother of a yellow and a
running up the mountain
to get before it happens
to the child who is a
bird who is a falling

OLD FRENCH MAN *is dreaming.*

l'oiseau blanc dans le metro
le chapeau dans le bateau

BIRDBOOK WOMAN *is dreaming.*

up
round
down
in

INSOMNIAC GAY *continues during this.*

11. Obsessive 2

US MAN *gets up again while dreaming is going on,*
starts rituals as before.

BUSINESSMAN *dreams.*

a cat who is a
woman with a furry and a
purring and a further and
further and a further and a
fury and a

US MAN *finishes rituals satisfactorily and goes back to*
bed.

Silence. Everyone is still.

12. Ghost

GHOST

It's me.
Let me into your sleep.
Let me in when you wake.
I've been dead so long
I've forgotten why
I've not gone away.

I walk out of the night
can't you hear
can't you see
it's me
I've forgotten who
I've forgotten why.

13. Dawn

Silence. But now and then a little sound from the insomniac.

OLD FRENCH WOMAN *wakes.*

OLD WOMAN
tous les matins
très bonne heure
j'ai peur de mourir
les oiseaux
j'ai peur

BIRDBOOK WOMAN *wakes.*

BIRDBOOK WOMAN
blackbird thrush starling wren

INSOMNIAC *falls asleep.*

OLD WOMAN *gets up.*

OLD WOMAN
je me lave
très bonne heure
j'n'ai plus peur
le matin
les oiseaux

14. Morning

BIRDBOOK WOMAN *gets up and dresses, takes birdbook and binoculars and goes out.*

BIRDBOOK WOMAN
blackbird

OLD WOMAN *makes tea and wakes* OLD MAN.

AFFAIR COUPLE *reprise 'your eyes' and goodbye goodbye.*

GAY 1 *wakes.* GAY 2, INSOMNIAC, *still sleeping.*

GAY 1
don't know what you want
but I want you
again

US MAN *wakes cheerful,* US WOMAN *still sleepy.*

US MAN
looks like a great day

US WOMAN
uh huh

US MAN
not a cloud in the sky

US WOMAN
uh huh

BUSINESSMAN *puts on TV.*

TV
after the break . . relationships expert . .

BUSINESSMAN *phones home.*

Hi darling . . big kiss

SILENT COUPLE *who have been asleep throughout
wake up.*

DRUNK COUPLE *waking up*

my head bang my belly bang my eyes bang my knees bang
my heart bang

OLD COUPLE
on va au fleuve
allons vite

OLD COUPLE *leave.*

AFFAIR WOMAN *leaves.*

AFFAIR MAN
your eyes
my angel
what if I lose

This becomes duet with GAY 1.
INSOMNIAC *still asleep.*
AFFAIR MAN *leaves.*

BUSINESSMAN
bacon and eggs and tomato and sausage and mushroom
and bacon

GAY 1 *joins in.*

BUSINESSMAN *leaves for breakfast.*

GAY 1 *can't wake* INSOMNIAC *so leaves for breakfast too.*

DRUNK COUPLE *manage to leave.*

SILENT COUPLE *leave.*

Nobody left but INSOMNIAC *asleep.*

The TV is still on.

TV
bright spells and scattered
clearing later
shaping up to be a nice
and over now to

TWO NIGHTS

From a diary found in a hotel room

Hand Gone

my hand has gone
january
very late at night
today my whole left side
six and a half minutes
disappeared

July

july
city out of sight in the haze
wish I could disappear
magician made the tower disappear from the ground up
and all the people who lived

Thin

thin and cold
the wind blows right through me

Mysterious Disappearance

mysterious disappearance

the judge said
any disappearance or loss
unknown puzzling baffling
hard to explain or understand
mysterious disappearance

a ring left on a dresser
later it's not there
no evidence of theft
the loss would be mysterious disappearance

Suddenly

suddenly at a party
ran out invisible and hid
saw myself slowly appear in the mirror on the wall in the
sauntered downstairs for a drink
'where have you been?'

try to stop fading but

or shall I try to disappear?

no good the way I am

Will to Power

the will to power as disappearance
it says
logical radical option for our time
it says
not a disaster not a death
but a way to what?

Shadow

will I still have a shadow?
will I still have a mind?
wind blow through
will invisible eyes still see?

Spell

the spell if I dare
here in a hotel room
eye of a nightowl
smear your whole body
say to Helios
by your great name
Zizia
Lailam
a a a a
I I I I
o o o o
ieo
in the presence of any man until sunset
make me invisible

Hand .. Light

held my hand up to the light and

A Nick Hern Book

Hotel first published in Great Britain in this special edition
in 1997 by Nick Hern Books Limited, 14 Larden Road,
London W3 7ST in association with Second Stride, London.

Hotel copyright © 1997 by Caryl Churchill

Quotes in the 'Will to Power section' from *TAZ*
by Hakim Bey, published by Autonomedia

Quotes in the 'Spell section' from *Greek Magical Papyri
including the Demotic Spells* by H. Dieter-Bitz, published
by the University of Chicago Press © 1986, 1992

Typeset by Country Setting, Woodchurch, Kent TN26 3TB
Printed by CLE Print Limited, St Ives, Cambs PE27 3LE

ISBN 978 1 85459 337 5

A CIP catalogue record for this book is available from
the British Library